Exceptional African Americans

# MAE JEMISON

## First African-American Woman in Space

**Charlotte Taylor**
**and**
**Stephen Feinstein**

Enslow Publishing
101 W. 23rd Street
Suite 240
New York, NY 10011
USA

enslow.com

# Words to Know

**astronaut**—A person who goes into space.

**chemistry**—The science that studies the basic parts of matter.

**engineering**—The study of how things work.

**experiment**—A test used to answer a question or make a discovery.

**NASA**—National Aeronautics and Space Administration. The group in charge of the United States space program.

**Peace Corps (CORE)**—A group of Americans who go all over the world to help other people.

**science fiction**—A made-up story based on scientific ideas.

**space shuttle**—A spaceship that moves people and things between Earth and space.

**volunteer**—To do work without being paid.

# Contents

For years, Mae Jemison dreamed of going into space. Here she is on the space shuttle *Endeavour*.

# CHAPTER 1

# A Curious Child

**When Mae Jemison** was only five years old, she told her teacher she wanted to be a scientist. Even though she was very young, Mae knew what she wanted. She worked hard and did not give up on her dream.

Mae Carol Jemison was born on October 17, 1956, in Decatur, Alabama. A few years later, her family moved to Chicago, Illinois.

Mae's mother, Dorothy, was a teacher. She and Mae's father, Charles, knew learning was important. They made sure that their children did well in school.

## Mae Says:

"My parents were the best scientists I knew, because they were always asking questions."

### A Love of Learning

When Mae was in first grade, she was ready to do science projects. She helped her big sister, Ada Sue, and her big brother, Ricky, with their science projects.

When Mae was in third grade, she finally got a science project of her own to do. It was all about how life on Earth started and how it changed over time. Mae worked on her science project all the way up to the sixth grade!

Mae was curious about the world. She read about dinosaurs. She found out about all kinds

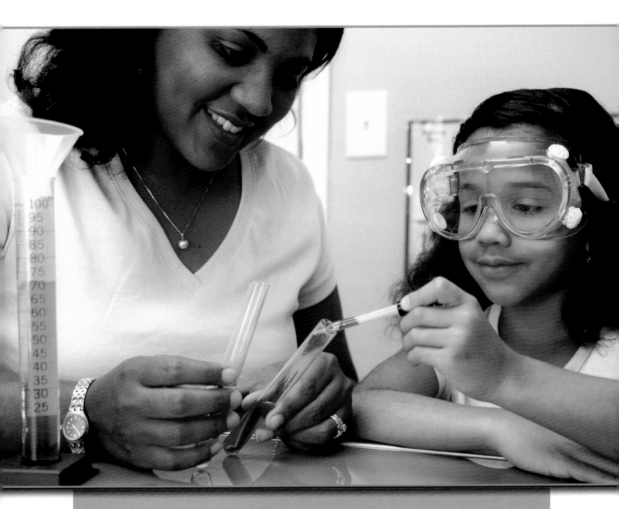

Like this girl, Mae enjoyed doing science projects.

of early plant and animal life. She also read about the stars and the planets. She often went to the library and stayed there until it closed. On the way home, she would look up at the stars twinkling in the sky. She wondered where they came from.

These children are looking at the stars, as Mae did when she was a young girl.

CHAPTER 2

# Faraway Worlds

**As Mae got older**, her dream of going into space grew stronger. She loved reading **science fiction** books about travel to other planets. It made her want to go to these places.

On July 20, 1969, **astronauts** Neil Armstrong, Buzz Aldrin, and Mike Collins became the first people to go to the moon. Mae was very excited. She read all about the moon landing. If only there were some way that she could become an astronaut too!

But there was a problem. So far, all the astronauts were white men. Would **NASA**—the National Aeronautics and Space Administration—ever choose an African-American woman to become an astronaut?

Mae Says:

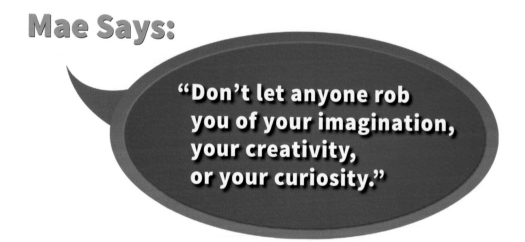

"Don't let anyone rob you of your imagination, your creativity, or your curiosity."

*Apollo 11* astronauts (left to right) Neil Armstrong, Mike Collins, and Buzz Aldrin. For many years, all astronauts were white men.

**Buzz Aldrin stands next to the American flag the astronauts put on the moon.**

# CHAPTER 3

# Dr. Jemison

**Mae knew** she had to do a lot of work before she could become an astronaut. At age sixteen, she was ready to begin college. Mae studied **chemistry** and **engineering** at Stanford University in California.

By the time she graduated in 1977, she had decided to become a doctor. She wanted to help people. So she went to medical school.

## Mae Helps Others

While studying to be a doctor, Mae did **volunteer** work in Africa and Asia. She took care of people in small villages.

Mae worked in villages like this one in Africa.

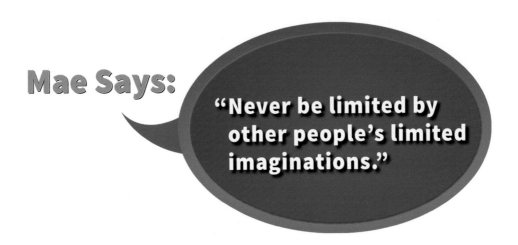

Mae Says:

"Never be limited by other people's limited imaginations."

In 1981, Mae became a doctor. First she worked in Los Angeles, California. The next year, she went back to Africa as a doctor in the **Peace Corps**. She helped people in Africa for several years. Then in 1985, Mae moved back to California.

# CHAPTER 4

# Mae Blasts Off

**Mae loved** her work as a doctor. But she never forgot her dream of becoming an astronaut.

In 1985, Mae finally got the chance she was hoping for. NASA was looking for new people to become astronauts.

Mae decided to try. Perhaps she now had a chance to be chosen. African-American men had already joined the space program. And in 1983, Sally Ride had become the first American woman to go into space. Maybe NASA was ready for an African-American woman astronaut.

On January 28, 1986, a terrible accident happened. The **space shuttle** *Challenger* blew up and crashed shortly after it took off. All the astronauts aboard were killed. Mae knew that going into space was dangerous. But she was not afraid. In February 1987, NASA chose Mae for the astronaut program.

Guion Bluford was the first African-American astronaut in space.

## A Trip to Space

Mae lived and worked at the Johnson Space Center in Houston, Texas, for five years. While training to be an astronaut, she learned all about the space shuttle. She studied many different science subjects.

On September 12, 1992, Mae blasted into space aboard the *Endeavour*. She was the first African-American woman in space. During her eight days in space, Mae did science **experiments**. She wanted to learn how to keep people healthy in space.

## A New Dream

After she returned to Earth, Mae had a new dream. She wanted to use science to make the world a better place. Mae left NASA in 1993 and started her own company.

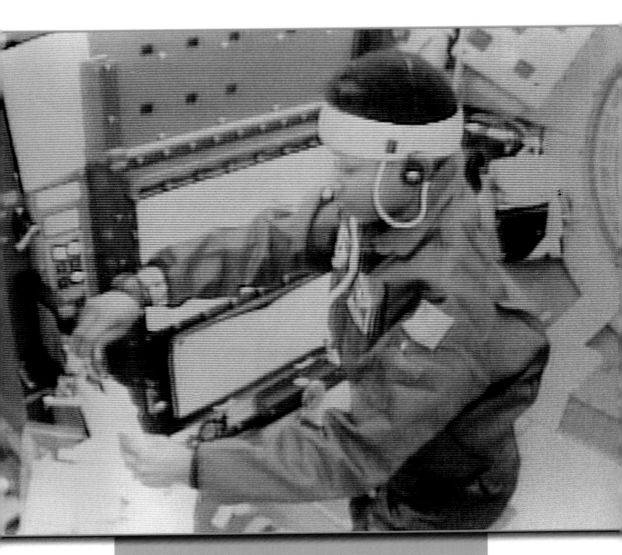

Mae did many experiments in space.

Mae gives speeches all around the country. Here she is speaking with NYC Police Athletic League summer campers in New York City.

To share her ideas, Mae taught science in college and gave speeches all around the country. She always told young people not to be afraid to follow their dreams.

## Mae Says:

"The thing that I have done throughout my life is to do the best job that I can and to be me."

Mae still loves learning about the stars and the planets. In 2012, she became the leader of the 100-Year Starship. This program was started to help us learn more about space travel. Mae is helping give others the chance to follow their dreams into space.

# Timeline

**1956**—Mae is born in Alabama on October 17.

**1977**—Mae graduates from Stanford University with a science degree.

**1981**—Mae gets a medical degree from Cornell University Medical College.

**1982**—Mae joins the Peace Corps in Africa.

**1987**—Mae is accepted into NASA's astronaut program.

**1992**—On September 12, Mae becomes the first African-American woman to go into space.

**1993**—Mae retires from NASA.

**1994**—Mae starts a company to take technology to other countries and to improve science education. She also founds The Earth We Share (TEWS), an international science camp for high school students.

**1995**—Mae begins teaching at Dartmouth College.

**2004**—Mae is inducted into the International Space Hall of Fame.

**2012**—Mae becomes the leader of the 100-Year Starship, a project to research space travel.

# Learn More

## Books

Jemison, Mae. *Discovering New Planets.* New York: Scholastic, 2013.

Jemison, Mae. *Journey Through Our Solar System.* New York: Scholastic, 2013.

Wheeler, Jill C. *Mae Jemison: Awesome Astronaut.* Edina, Minn.: ABDO, 2012.

## Web Sites

**teacher.scholastic.com/space/mae_jemison/index.htm**

Provides a brief biography of Jemison along with a timeline of events in space exploration.

**drmae.com**

The official Mae Jemison Web site includes timeline, current projects, biography, and FAQs.

**nasa.gov/audience/forkids/kidsclub/flash/index.html**

Includes interactive games, puzzles, and other space-related activities.

# Index

Published in 2016 by Enslow Publishing, LLC.
101 W. 23rd Street, Suite 240, New York, NY 10011

Copyright © 2016 by Enslow Publishing, LLC.

**Library of Congress Cataloging-in-Publication Data**

Taylor, Charlotte, 1978-
 Mae Jemison : first African-American woman in space / Charlotte Taylor and Stephen Feinstein.
  pages cm. — (Exceptional African Americans)
 Summary: "A biography of NASA astronaut Mae Jemison"— Provided by publisher.
 Includes bibliographical references and index.
 Audience: 8-up.
 Audience: Grades 4 to 6.
 ISBN 978-0-7660-6664-9 (library binding)
 ISBN 978-0-7660-6662-5 (pbk.)
 ISBN 978-0-7660-6663-2 (6-pack)
 1. Jemison, Mae, 1956—Juvenile literature. 2. African American women astronauts—Biography—Juvenile literature. 3. Astronauts—United States—Biography—Juvenile literature. I. Feinstein, Stephen. II. Title.
 TL789.85.J46T39 2016
 629.450092—dc23
 [B]
                    2015007442

Printed in the United States of America

**To Our Readers:** We have done our best to make sure all Web site addresses in this book were active and appropriate when we went to press. However, the author and the publisher have no control over and assume no liability for the material available on those Web sites or on any Web sites they may link to. Any comments or suggestions can be sent by e-mail to customerservice@enslow.com.

**Photo Credits:** ©AP Images: p. 19; PRNewsFoto/Bayer Corporation), p. 20; Getty Images: Science & Society Picture Library/SSPL, p. 1; Stuart O'Sullivan, p. 8; NASA, pp. 4, 11, 12, 17; Shutterstock.com: ©Toria (blue background throughout book); ©Rob Marmion, p. 7; ©Anton Ivanov, p. 14.

**Cover Credits:** Science & Society Picture Library/SSPL/Getty Images (portrait of Mae Jemison); ©Toria/Shutterstock.com (blue background).